W9-CHS-942

THE
AUTOBIOGRAPHY
OF
MALCOLM X

Malcolm X & Alex Haley

EDITORIAL DIRECTOR Justin Kestler
EXECUTIVE EDITOR Ben Florman
DIRECTOR OF TECHNOLOGY Tammy Hepps

SERIES EDITORS John Crowther, Justin Kestler
MANAGING EDITOR Vince Janoski

WRITER Ross Douthat, Brian Phillips
EDITOR Boomie Aglietti, John Crowther

Copyright © 2003 by SparkNotes LLC

All rights reserved. No part of this book may be used or reproduced in any manner
whatsoever without the written permission of the Publisher.

SPARKNOTES is a registered trademark of SparkNotes LLC

This edition published by Spark Publishing

Spark Publishing
A Division of SparkNotes LLC
120 Fifth Avenue, 8th Floor
New York, NY 10011

Any book purchased without a cover is stolen property, reported as "unsold and
destroyed" to the Publisher, who receives no payment for such "stripped books."

First edition.

Please submit all comments and questions or report errors to www.sparknotes.com/errors

Library of Congress Catalog-in-Publication Data available upon request

Printed and bound in the United States

ISBN 1-58663-833-5

Introduction:
Stopping to Buy SparkNotes on a Snowy Evening

Whose words these are you *think* you know.
Your paper's due tomorrow, though;
We're glad to see you stopping here
To get some help before you go.

Lost your course? You'll find it here.
Face tests and essays without fear.
Between the words, good grades at stake:
Get great results throughout the year.

Once school bells caused your heart to quake
As teachers circled each mistake.
Use SparkNotes and no longer weep,
Ace every single test you take.

Yes, books are lovely, dark, and deep,
But only what you grasp you keep,
With hours to go before you sleep,
With hours to go before you sleep.

CONTENTS

CONTEXT

MALCOLM X WAS BORN in Omaha, Nebraska, on May 19, 1925, and spent much of his life fighting for equal rights for African Americans. Freedom for African Americans was supposed to have come with the end of the Civil War in 1865, but their struggle to attain equality persisted well into the next century, and continues today. Despite freed slaves' legal and political gains during the period just after the Civil War, known as Reconstruction, they and their children suffered blows to their rights in the last decades of the nineteenth century. For example, in the case of *Plessy* v. *Ferguson,* the U.S. Supreme Court ruled that segregation, in the form of "separate but equal" public facilities, was constitutional. Legalized racism across America, especially in the South, continued through the first half of the twentieth century.

Suffering from discrimination, economic oppression, and violence at the hands of whites, African-American communities rallied around several different political leaders. Booker T. Washington (1856–1915) encouraged blacks to gain political power by earning the respect of white people through hard work and humble conduct. W.E.B. DuBois (1868–1963) demanded political empowerment and spiritual rebirth. Marcus Garvey (1887–1940) urged a return to Africa, contending that black people should rely upon their own unity and create their own means of empowerment. Garvey's fiercely nationalist ideas influenced many African Americans, among them Earl Little, Malcolm X's father, a preacher who spread Garvey's ideas in his small Michigan community.

During the Civil Rights movement of the 1960s, Malcolm X gained national and international prominence. Often distancing himself from the movement's leaders, he was perhaps the most controversial leader of the period. Malcolm X's separatism and militancy contrasted with the desegregation efforts and nonviolent tactics of Martin Luther King, Jr. Historians credit Malcolm X as the spiritual father of the Black Power movement of the late 1960s. At the time of Malcolm X's murder in 1965, his views and commitments were undergoing a great change. He was demanding unity and self-determination for black people, whose struggle he viewed in the context of oppressed peoples all over the world. He was also abandoning the hard-line anti–white prejudice of his early years.

The Autobiography of Malcolm X is the result of a collaboration between Malcolm X and journalist Alex Haley. Over a period of several years, Malcolm X told Haley his life story in a series of lengthy interviews. Haley wrote down and arranged the material in the first person, and Malcolm X edited and approved every chapter. Thus, though Haley actually did the writing, it is reasonable to consider the work an autobiography. The work is one of the most important nonfiction books of the twentieth century, as it offers valuable insight into the mind of a key figure on a core issue of twentieth-century America. In 1965, a New York reviewer wrote of Malcolm X, "No man has better expressed his people's trapped anguish." The autobiography continues to be relevant to efforts to combat racism. Equal rights activists fighting against oppression of African Americans revived Malcolm X's philosophy in the 1980s, and Spike Lee released the movie *Malcolm X* in 1992, shortly after the infamous beating of black motorist Rodney King by white police officers.

PLOT OVERVIEW

MALCOLM X IS BORN MALCOLM LITTLE in Omaha, Nebraska. The Midwest, during this period, is full of discrimination and racial violence. Malcolm's family moves to Michigan where they continue to experience persecution and violence. White people murder Malcolm's father and force his mother into a mental hospital. After living in a Michigan detention home and completing the eighth grade, Malcolm moves to Boston, Massachusetts, to live with his half-sister, Ella. In Boston Malcolm quickly becomes involved in urban nightlife. He passes for being much older than he is, wearing flashy clothes, gambling, drinking, doing drugs, and dating an older white woman, Sophia. Malcolm eventually takes a job as a railway porter. He then moves to New York, where he begins working as a hustler in Harlem. Malcolm's various jobs there include running numbers, selling drugs, and steering white people to black brothels. He also commits armed robberies.

When life in Harlem becomes too dangerous, Malcolm returns to Boston, where he becomes a house burglar and is eventually arrested. In prison, Malcolm transforms himself, converting to the branch of Islam promoted by the Nation of Islam, which has already converted a number of Malcolm's siblings. Inspired by the faith, Malcolm stops using drugs; he reads voraciously, prays, studies English and Latin, and joins the prison debate team.

The prison releases Malcolm on parole. Malcolm moves in with his brother Wilfred and becomes very active in the Detroit temple of the Nation of Islam. Malcolm receives permission to drop his last name, which a white slave owner gave to one of his ancestors. He adopts the placeholder "X" as his last name, using the letter to represent the lost name of his African ancestors. Malcolm X soon meets the Nation of Islam's leader, Elijah Muhammad, and rises quickly from the rank of temple assistant in Detroit to the Nation's first national minister. Malcolm X becomes known throughout the United States, even outside of Muslim circles, as a fiery advocate for black unity and militancy. The Nation of Islam's leaders resent and fear Malcolm despite his allegiance to their cause, and they suspend him from the organization.

The Nation of Islam's frustration with Malcolm intensifies, and Malcolm begins receiving death threats. After a divisive argument with Elijah Muhammad, Malcolm leaves the Nation of Islam. He uses his fame to found his own organization, Muslim Mosque, Inc. He sees his organization as more politically active than the Nation of Islam. On a trip to the Middle East and Africa, Malcolm discovers what he sees as true Islam. This version of Islam contrasts with the version of Islam he has been teaching. By the end of his life, Malcolm X is an international figure, welcomed by foreign leaders and committed to Islam as a religion that can alleviate the racial problems of the United States. He is assassinated in 1965.

CHARACTER LIST

Malcolm X (also known as Malcolm Little, Detroit Red, and El Hajj Malik El-Shabazz)   The narrator and subject of the autobiography. As a young boy Malcolm is bright and popular but feels excluded by white people. He becomes a ruthless hustler on the streets of Boston and New York but undergoes a change of heart during his time in prison. After his release, he develops into an aggressive and persuasive spokesman for the Nation of Islam. As an independent and international political leader, he is tolerant, meditative, and ambitious.

Elijah Muhammad   The spiritual leader of the Nation of Islam. Malcolm treats Elijah with immense respect even before he knows him, writing him letters daily while still in prison. Though he seems like a benevolent father figure, Elijah Muhammad becomes a jealous and defensive leader as his health fails and as Malcolm becomes more powerful.

Sister Betty   Malcolm's wife, a quiet and strong woman. The autobiography does not emphasize Betty's role, though she acts as Malcolm's secretary, housekeeper, and confidante. Betty endures his busy traveling and work schedule, gives birth to five of his children, and witnesses his assassination.

Shorty   Malcolm's best friend during his Boston years. Shorty is a musician who at first leads and then follows Malcolm into a life of crime. Shorty is a foil for Malcolm: while Malcolm converts to an aggressive hustler lifestyle, Shorty leads a comparatively normal life. The differences between the two men is clear in Shorty's surprise at Malcolm's foul language and violent tendencies, which he witnesses when Malcolm returns to Boston from New York.

Ella Little Malcolm's half-sister on his father's side. When Malcolm is an adolescent, Ella provides him with a model of female strength and black pride. She represents family unity within the autobiography. She welcomes Malcolm into her home in Boston and always supports him, later lending him money for his pilgrimage to Mecca.

Earl Little Malcolm's father. A preacher and political organizer from Georgia, Earl is a tall and outspoken authority figure in Malcolm's early years. Earl's assassination by whites for preaching the Black Nationalist ideas of Marcus Garvey makes him a martyr for black nationalism.

Louise Little Malcolm's fair-skinned, black mother, who endures the worst of the Great Depression. For Malcolm, Louise represents the harm that the white government does even when it claims to be acting charitably. Welfare agents separate Louise from her children and put her in a mental hospital, and Malcolm's insistence on visiting her regularly shows his strong commitment to her.

Sophia Malcolm's white girlfriend. Malcolm and Sophia do not love each other but rather use each other as status symbols. Sophia represents the tempting allure of white women for black men, and the emptiness of her relationship with Malcolm shapes Malcolm's skepticism about interracial romance.

Laura Malcolm's first date, a quiet, middle-class black girl from Roxbury Hill. When Malcolm dumps Laura for Sophia, Laura becomes involved with drugs and prostitution. Laura is an innocent victim of the ruthless and self-hating behavior that Malcolm observes in urban black communities.

Sammy the Pimp A Harlem pimp and drug dealer. As close friends, Malcolm and Sammy work together until tension develops between them over Malcolm's assault on one of Sammy's girlfriends. This episode shows that even the closest friendships easily crumble when gambling, drugs, and violence are involved.

West Indian Archie An older Harlem hustler. Archie pays Malcolm for helping him run an informal gambling system in Harlem until they break violently over a misunderstanding. Archie's photographic memory and aptitude in math exemplify the wasted potential of the black ghetto.

Bimbi A prison inmate. Bimbi, the most vocal of Malcolm's fellow inmates, makes speeches that gain him the respect of guards and prisoners alike. He demonstrates to Malcolm the power of independent thought and persuasive argument, and thus serves as an inspiration to Malcolm when Malcolm converts to Islam.

Cassius Clay (Muhammad Ali) The world heavyweight boxing champion. Generous and understanding, Clay provides a place for Malcolm to stay during the first days of Malcolm's split from the Nation of Islam.

Reginald Little Malcolm's younger brother. Malcolm takes Reginald under his wing from an early age and continues to protect him in Harlem. Malcolm's later justification of Reginald's eventual insanity as retribution for sinning shows Malcolm's commitment to the principles of Islam.

ANALYSIS OF MAJOR CHARACTERS

Malcolm is the only major character in the autobiography. Though many characters play a role in the development of Malcolm's beliefs and career, the autobiography does not explore these characters in depth. This lack of attention to other characters is not surprising, as an autobiography always focuses primarily on one person. Malcolm, however, changes frequently during his lifetime. The various names by which he goes— Malcolm Little, Detroit Red, Satan, Malcolm X, and El-Hajj Malik El-Shabazz—correspond to the various phases of his life.

MALCOLM AS MALCOLM LITTLE

Malcolm Little passively endures the experiences that motivate his later obsession with racial politics in America. He encounters open racism when whites murder his father and subtle racism when white welfare agents institutionalize his mother. Though Malcolm endures this racism quietly, it leads to his later development of anti-white views. He ambitiously attempts to integrate himself into his predominantly white junior high school, but his white teachers' and classmates' racism thwarts his development. Attempting to flee the racist Midwest, Malcolm moves to Boston but finds racist dynamics exaggerated in the large coastal cities. These early frustrations at the hands of a society unwilling to accept his efforts to fit in build a separatist fervor in Malcolm.

MALCOLM AS DETROIT RED

The lifestyle of Detroit Red, the name Malcolm adopts as a hustler, illuminates the moral decay plaguing the ghetto. Fresh from Michigan, young Malcolm Little quickly adopts zoot suits, slang, drugs, and gambling, showing how easy it is to be seduced by fast-paced nightlife. Earning the nickname "Detroit Red" for his bright red hair, he learns to conduct business and ruthlessly fend for himself, laying the ground for his later argument that living in the ghetto encourages deceit and destruction. Detroit Red has few ethical restraints but many social insights. His philosophy requires that he trust no one, know his enemy well, and carefully defend his public image. Detroit Red represents the fact that many black people struggle just to survive.

MALCOLM AS SATAN

In prison, after earning the nickname "Satan" for his foul temper and preference for solitary confinement, Malcolm starts educating himself and turns his outlook around. His transformation begins when he gives himself up peacefully to a Boston detective, letting five years of street hustling catch up with him. This episode demonstrates the ideal of submission to moral authority, which Malcolm later embraces in a Muslim context to justify his willing subordination to Elijah Muhammad, the leader of the Nation of Islam. His embracing of Islam transforms him from a hustler interested in earning money any way he can into a responsible individual interested in educating and enriching himself. Malcolm's time in prison thus represents the transition between his early years of suffering and deceit and his later years of faith and activism.

MALCOLM AS MALCOLM X

As Minister Malcolm X, Malcolm develops confidence and credibility as a religious leader and media personality. Malcolm carefully shapes the identity and significance of this persona. As he rises in the ranks of the Nation of Islam to take over from the ailing Elijah Muhammad, the press pays close attention to his philosophies, allowing him to disseminate his message widely. Although his public statements do not initially depart from the Nation of Islam's party line, Malcolm eventually begins to broaden his message to address white America. As the shock-value media personality Malcolm X, he calls for a more active approach to domestic racial politics, and his influence in American society shows the effectiveness with which he has shaped his persona. After a trip to Africa, Malcolm X counsels blacks to align themselves with the nonwhite majority internationally, illustrating his general tendency to let the wisdom he gains from his experiences influence his attitudes.

Malcolm as El-Hajj Malik El-Shabazz

When Malcolm leaves the Nation of Islam, he adopts the name El-Hajj Malik El-Shabazz and begins arguing for worldwide racial tolerance. Though Malcolm, as El-Shabazz, claims that his rapid turnaround to racial tolerance in Mecca is due to the "colorblindness" of the Muslim societies of Egypt and Saudi Arabia, the events in the autobiography foreshadow Malcolm's change of heart. Even as Malcolm X, Malcolm begins to question the extremist message of the Nation of Islam. Malcolm's decision to take the title El-Hajj after making the pilgrimage to Mecca (a religious duty called "*hajj*" in Arabic) symbolizes his faith in international Islam. Additionally, his calls for white groups to work for racial justice and his attempts to integrate the struggles of black Americans with the struggles of oppressed nonwhite peoples everywhere reveal how his perspective on race relations has matured. Whereas Malcolm's earlier political activism, such as his militant advocacy of black separatism, is marked by hostility, his later activism seeks to create racial harmony.

CHARACTER ANALYSIS

THEMES, MOTIFS & SYMBOLS

THEMES

THEMES

Themes are the fundamental and often universal ideas explored in a literary work.

MALCOLM'S CHANGING PERSPECTIVE ON RACISM

Malcolm's changing views of America's racial problems reflect the development of his character. When, as a child, he sees both of his parents destroyed by white society, he feels despair about the plight of blacks. His attitude changes, however, after his experiences in the black ghettos of Boston and New York develop in him the philosophy that black people should not accept help from white people. The teachings of the Nation of Islam that he receives in prison effect a further change in both Malcolm's character and his view of white people. He simultaneously abandons his wild past and embraces a systematic hatred of whites. His later travels in the Middle East cause another profound change; his break from the American Nation of Islam coincides with his newfound belief that blacks will be successful in their struggle for equal rights only if they identify with oppressed peoples across the globe. His attitude at the end of the work contrasts with his previous beliefs in that he now supports white participation in the struggle for black emancipation, whereas he earlier does not. Only after passing through so many phases and seeing the race problem from so many different perspectives is Malcolm able to settle on a philosophy in which he truly believes.

THE SIMILARITY BETWEEN HUSTLING AND ACTIVISM

Though Malcolm gives up gambling, smoking, and crime while in prison, his experience as an evangelist after prison is similar in ways to his earlier experience as a hustler. Malcolm retains insights, skills, and values from his years as a hustler that serve him in his later role as a religious authority and media personality. For example, Malcolm uses the knowledge he gains in Harlem—to distrust people, to know his enemies, and to craft his public image carefully—in his dealings with the Nation of Islam and with the press. Near the end of his life, Malcolm jokes to a university audience that he took his bachelor's degree on the streets of Harlem. This comment emphasizes the usefulness of the skills that he gained while living a life of hustling. Though he now condemns his former lifestyle, his words show that he appreciates what that lifestyle taught him about how to interact with people effectively. The skills Malcolm uses as a hustler and later as an activist are not developed with these future roles in mind, but rather are built upon the necessary survival skills that Malcolm learned at a young age, emphasizing that life is a matter of survival for the urban black man. Though Malcolm's young life is very different from his adult life, his ability to fight for survival in America's racist culture is equally important at both stages of his life.

HUMANITY AS A BASIC RIGHT

In *The Autobiography of Malcolm X,* Malcolm focuses on how racism against blacks dehumanizes them. The white people around Malcolm often view him as something less than human, and Malcolm's desire to correct this perception drives his fight for racial equality. He experiences subtle racism in his youth from his family and school, who treat him differently from others because he is black. Though his foster parents and some of the people he encounters in school are nice to him, Malcolm thinks these people treat him nicely in order to show how unprejudiced they are. He feels that they are using him because he is different, as though he were a "pink poodle." Malcolm in turn dehumanizes certain white people as revenge for his own subjugation. In Boston, he displays his white girlfriend Sophia as a status symbol, viewing her less as a person than as an enviable object that he owns. However, when after many years of anti–white rhetoric in the Nation of Islam, Malcolm meets white-skinned people in Mecca who treat him as an equal, he begins to acknowledge the humanity of individual whites.

MOTIFS

> *Motifs are recurring structures, contrasts, or literary devices that can help to develop and inform the text's major themes.*

STATUS SYMBOLS

In *The Autobiography of Malcolm X,* characters often associate with other people just to be seen with them, treating them like objects rather than human beings. The autobiography points out this habit to show how society's hierarchy of status determines our identities and sense of self-worth. Malcolm first experiences this hierarchy when he gets special treatment from his father because he is the lightest-skinned of his siblings. His father's preferential treatment illustrates how Malcolm's superficial traits, rather than his personality, give him priority within the hierarchy of his family. When Malcolm's Michigan foster family treats him as special and his school elects him class president, Malcolm is at first proud but later resentful of being a "mascot" for white ideals of how blacks should behave. Neither his school nor his foster family recognizes Malcolm as a person. Rather, they use Malcolm's skin color to demonstrate their apparent tolerance and broadmindedness, and thereby gain status for themselves. Malcolm himself uses his white girlfriend Sophia as just such a status symbol, parading her like a new car for his jealous and gawking friends at Boston bars. Much later, Elijah Muhammad uses Malcolm X as a symbol of the Nation of Islam's vitality as well as a strategic resource in growing his organization. In each case a person is degraded to the status of an object in the service of someone else's social advancement.

Travel and Transformation

The autobiography links instances of travel and transformation to show the simultaneous physical and spiritual aspects of Malcolm's changes. Malcolm undergoes several quick and total conversions, and each involves first traveling to a distant, confusing place. In his travels, Malcolm is searching for both a home and a philosophy. When he moves to Boston, he quickly absorbs the activities of those around him, taking up lavish street-style zoot suits, marijuana, jazz, gambling, and petty crime. Similarly, in prison he begins to emulate intelligent and reflective prisoners, such as Bibi, and eventually reinvents himself as a worldly individual and devoted Muslim. When he is expelled from the Nation of Islam and makes the pilgrimage to Mecca, not knowing Arabic or local customs, Malcolm greatly broadens his perspective on race in America by incorporating the wisdom he gains from his experiences into his philosophy. The period of travel that always precedes Malcolm's major conversions shows the influence of Malcolm's environment on his worldview and his eagerness for his views to be as informed as possible.

MOTIFS

SYMBOLS

Symbols are objects, characters, figures, or colors used to represent abstract ideas or concepts.

THE CONK

The conk, a popular hairstyle that involves straightening out nappy hair with a host of caustic chemicals, is an emblem of black self-denial. Blacks conk their hair in an attempt to look more like white people, and their willingness to alter a feature of their body violently underscores how much they want to conceal their blackness. The conk is popular with rich and poor blacks alike, showing how blacks of all classes experience self-hatred. Though Malcolm conks his hair when he first moves to Boston, in prison he realizes how much mental energy he has been wasting on trying to conform to an impossible image of white good looks. Later, as an orator canvassing on the street, Malcolm criticizes American blacks for trying to change their African features. He sees the conk as one item in a long list, including faith in Christian religion and obsession with white women, of counterproductive black imitations of white culture.

THE WATCH, SUITCASE, AND EYEGLASSES

The wristwatch, suitcase, and eyeglasses that Malcolm purchases upon his release from prison symbolize his commitment as a free man to a career of efficient work, frequent travel to spread the message of Islam, and constant study and reflection. The watch represents Malcolm's industriousness, as he becomes extremely conscious of his daily schedule and organizes his life carefully. The suitcase, which Malcolm begins using in his professional life, represents Malcolm's sacrifice of his personal life to his aspirations in the Nation of Islam. The glasses represent his ongoing commitment to the further development of his views as well as his broad vision for the future of black people in America.

SUMMARY & ANALYSIS

CHAPTERS ONE & TWO

SUMMARY—CHAPTER ONE: NIGHTMARE

When Malcolm Little's mother is pregnant with Malcolm, hooded Ku Klux Klan members break the windows of his family's house in Omaha, Nebraska. The white supremacists' target is Malcolm's father, Earl Little, a tall, black Baptist preacher from Georgia, because he works for Marcus Garvey's Universal Negro Improvement Association (UNIA), which supports the return of American blacks to Africa. Malcolm is Earl's seventh and lightest-skinned child. He is the only son who escapes Earl's beatings and gets to follow his father to UNIA meetings. Malcolm's mother, Louise Little, is a fair-skinned, educated woman from the island of Grenada. She was conceived when her father, a white man she never knew, raped her mother. Though Louise is able to get domestic work in town by passing as white, she stays at home to cook and clean for her family.

When the family moves to Lansing, Michigan, in 1929, another white supremacist group burns down their house. Malcolm says that watching his house burn taught him one of many early lessons about being black in America. He sees that success for blacks in Lansing means waiting tables or shining shoes rather than working in a respected profession and that the majority of black people are poor and jobless. After a white boy cheats Malcolm out of a hard-earned dollar, Malcolm realizes that the odds are stacked against blacks. However, Malcolm also learns some positive lessons. After making a fuss at home gets him extra biscuits, Malcolm concludes that the way to get something is to ask for it.

When Malcolm is six, white men who oppose Earl's black nationalist work kill him. Earl's life insurance company refuses to pay what it owes the family, claiming that Earl's death was a suicide. The Great Depression is on, and with only dandelions to eat, the Little family is forced to rely on welfare. When Malcolm steals food from stores, welfare agents blame Louise. They call her crazy for rejecting free pork because she wants to adhere to Seventh Day Adventist dietary restrictions. When social workers send Louise to a mental hospital, the kids split up and all but the eldest two go to foster homes. Malcolm blames the state welfare agency for robbing his mother of her dignity and breaking apart his family.

SUMMARY—CHAPTER TWO: MASCOT

In 1937 Malcolm moves in with the Swerlins, a white foster family in Lansing. He accepts their generosity, but feels more like a "mascot" or a pet than a human being equal to those around him. Malcolm is first in his class at Mason Junior High, but he does not feel comfortable at school. Though he is proud when the students elect him class president, he feels like a "pink poodle"—more of an oddity than a human being. In history class Malcolm finds only one paragraph on black history in the textbook. The teacher laughs as he tells Malcolm's class that though the slaves have been freed, black people are still lazy and dumb. Malcolm tells his English teacher, Mr. Ostrowski, that he wants to become a lawyer. Though Mr. Ostrowski supports the professional aspirations of white students who are less intelligent than Malcolm, he tells Malcolm to become a carpenter. Malcolm comes to resent his white school and home, and realizes that even well-meaning white people do not see black people as their equals.

Malcolm grows up quickly, and racial barriers often frustrate him. He bristles when people call him "coon" and "nigger" on the basketball court. He gets a job washing dishes, and he sometimes visits his mother at the mental hospital. He also visits his brothers and sisters, who live in different cities. On weekends, he dances to swing music at bars, where he sees interracial romances that cannot occur openly in Lansing. White boys pressure Malcolm to ask out white girls, but he realizes they just want a dirty secret to hold over the girls' heads.

Malcolm spends the summer of 1940 in Boston, visiting his half-sister, Ella. She is a strong black woman with a deep sense of family loyalty. Frustrated by how he has been treated at school and at home, Malcolm decides to move to Boston. The Swerlins do not understand why Malcolm wants to leave, and Malcolm is not able to explain his motivation to them. He moves into an upstairs room in Ella's house in Roxbury, a wealthy black neighborhood in Boston. He is glad to move away, later speculating that if he had stayed in Lansing, he would have gotten a menial job or become a complacent middle-class lawyer. Though only fifteen, he can pass for several years older, and he begins to look for a job.

ANALYSIS — CHAPTERS ONE & TWO

Malcolm's experience of racial prejudice from both white and black people shows the extent to which racism is ingrained in society. Malcolm's father, Earl, who spends his days working to help black people support themselves and return to Africa, is one of the last people we would expect to hold racist views. But he treats Malcolm better than he treats his other sons because Malcolm has the lightest skin. Malcolm learns by witnessing his parents' fates that racist double standards are a serious problem in his society. His father is killed by a group of whites for promoting a strong, independent black community, and his mother is driven crazy by a white welfare agency that does not trust her to take care of her children because she is black. Although Malcolm's light skin makes it possible for him to be accepted by the Swerlins and elected class president of Mason Junior High, he continues to experience discrimination. The Swerlins treat him like a pet, and his school discourages him from pursuing his dream to be a lawyer. Malcolm cannot escape the atmosphere of racial prejudice, as it pervades everything from the welfare agencies and his school to his family relationships.

Earl Little struggles against a moral double standard that illustrates the hypocrisy of white society in the 1930s. White society of this time allows blacks to succeed so long as their success doesn't affect white America. The fact that Earl meets no resistance in his career as a Christian preacher shows that whites consider him harmless to their society. Though the Midwest generally respects religious figures such as preachers, Earl's success does not indicate that white people look to him for moral guidance. Rather, they allow him to succeed only because he is professing mainstream Christian views. As soon as Earl espouses Marcus Garvey's separatist ideals and thereby goes against mainstream society, white people turn against him, breaking his windows, burning down his house, and ultimately killing him. Earl's fate shows that white society allows black people to succeed, but only so long as they do not challenge the established order.

The experiences of Malcolm's mother, Louise, illustrate the problems that arise when an individual does not fit neatly into established social categories. Louise's light skin allows her to pass as black or white, but she is not fully comfortable in either world. We might think that Louise's ability to pass as white would give her a social advantage, but while she can get housework jobs in town, her employers fire her when they discover that she is black. Although the housework jobs allow her to support her family, in order to maintain these jobs Louise must deny her black heritage, and she loses her jobs anyway. Once her husband is murdered, she has no choice but to accept the assistance that the white welfare agencies offer and to endure the loss of self-respect and control that goes with receiving such assistance. In many ways, Louise's light skin makes her life harder rather than easier. Her dual heritage makes her an outsider to both of her cultures.

For Malcolm, growing up means learning to navigate the paradoxes that being black in a racist society creates for him. As the lightest-skinned of his siblings, he finds that some doors are open to him, as they are for his mother, but that many more remain closed. As a young boy, he can shoot raccoons, play basketball, and work as a dishwasher. Though he experiences some freedom, the nature of these activities shows that white society still considers him an inferior. On the street, white boys encourage him to ask out white girls, but he knows that if he touches them, he may be lynched. The illusion that he is able to choose any girlfriend he wishes is crushed by his knowledge that society considers mixed-race relationships taboo. Similarly, that Malcolm earns the number one rank in his class and becomes class president shows that the school system allows him to succeed to an extent. But his English teacher's comment that Malcolm should become a carpenter rather than a lawyer demonstrates that whites are willing to allow black success only to a certain point. The school allows Malcolm to become class president largely because it wants to avoid the appearance of being openly racist. Malcolm comes to understand, however, that white society bestows privilege on him only when doing so doesn't threaten the established order of white society.

Malcolm's comment that he feels like a "pink poodle" expresses his feeling of being excluded from mainstream society, which sees him as a cute, harmless, and ultimately expendable being. A single black student in a mostly white school is like a poodle in a human family: a tame, obedient creature that represents no real threat to anyone. Society views Malcolm as a novelty rather than as a real person with real goals, and it wants him to obey his masters—whites—like a poodle. A black student achieving well in school is seen simply as a rarer breed of poodle. That Malcolm sees himself as a *pink* poodle reinforces his feelings of emasculation; white oppression strips him of the power and independence he would normally feel as a man. Malcolm realizes that no level of achievement or popularity will break down the fundamental barrier to his acceptance and success in society: his race. In his foster family, just as in school, Malcolm is able to fit in as a "mascot," but not as a person. He is paraded as white society's ideal for how blacks should behave, but white society does not consider him a human being in his own right.

CHAPTERS THREE & FOUR

SUMMARY—CHAPTER THREE: HOMEBOY

Malcolm arrives in Boston looking like a country person without any sense of urban fashion. He lives with his half-sister, Ella, who encourages him to explore the city before tying himself down to a job. Malcolm quickly sees the difference between the pace and lifestyle of Boston and that of Lansing. He also sees a difference between the lifestyle of the middle-class blacks who, like Ella, live in the neighborhood of Roxbury Hill, and that of ghetto blacks, who have less money and live further down the hill. Malcolm is drawn to the latter, objecting to the ways in which the "Hill Negroes" try to imitate white people and glorify their own menial jobs. When Malcolm finally begins to look for a job, he begins frequenting a pool hall and befriends one employee there, Shorty. Shorty, who turns out to be from Lansing as well, works at the hall racking balls and tending tables, but he is also an aspiring saxophonist with contacts all over town. Shorty immediately takes Malcolm under his wing, giving him pocket money and arranging a job for him.

At the Roseland State Ballroom, where all the big bands perform, Malcolm replaces the shoeshine boy, who has just won the local numbers racket, an unofficial lottery played for small amounts of money. The outgoing shoeshine boy trains Malcolm in the basics of the job, which include tending the men's restroom, passing out towels, selling condoms, and shining shoes. Malcolm soon learns that much of the job's income actually comes from selling alcohol and marijuana, and acting as a go-between for black pimps and white customers. Malcolm begins to shoot craps, play cards, gamble, drink, smoke, and use drugs. With his earnings, he buys his first zoot suit, a flamboyant outfit fashionable on the street. He also gets his first "conk," a hairstyle in which one's hair is chemically straightened and flattened. At parties, Malcolm overcomes his shyness and develops a great passion for dancing. He contrasts the unadventurous dancing done in Michigan with the expressive dancing that goes on at the Boston parties. Malcolm eventually quits his ballroom job and makes his first appearance at the Roseland as a customer.

SUMMARY — CHAPTER FOUR: LAURA

Ella gets Malcolm a job as a clerk at a drugstore in Roxbury Hill. Malcolm hates the middle-class atmosphere, but one patron named Laura, a studious high school student, stands out from the others. Once his friendship with her develops, Malcolm confesses to Laura his old dream of becoming a lawyer, which she encourages. Laura is an excellent dancer, but she has a protective grandmother, whom she must lie to and fight with in order to go out dancing. The second time Malcolm and Laura go dancing, they compete in a dance-off at the Roseland, winning over the crowd and even the bandleader, the legendary Duke Ellington.

Malcolm attracts the attention of a white woman, Sophia, and dances with her. He takes Laura home and then returns to the Roseland and eventually leaves with Sophia in her convertible. Malcolm soon dumps Laura and begins to date Sophia. Sophia has white boyfriends in addition to Malcolm, but Malcolm keeps her as a status symbol. By dating an attractive white woman who is not a prostitute, Malcolm becomes something of a celebrity at nightclubs and bars. When Ella finds out about Sophia, she disapproves. Malcolm decides to move in with Shorty. Over the next few years, Malcolm hears about Laura's falling out with her grandmother, her introduction to drugs, and her stint as a prostitute. Looking back, Malcolm blames himself for ruining Laura's life.

ANALYSIS — CHAPTERS THREE & FOUR

This section shows how Malcolm's strong criticism of prejudice *within* the black community develops early in his life. Malcolm finds irony in the quickness of Roxbury Hill blacks to judge each other and inflate their own status in artificial ways. At a young age, Malcolm identifies the hypocrisy of his neighbors' tendency to judge each other on the basis of age, home ownership, and length of residency in New England, rather than on the basis of individual actions or character. Though "Hill Negroes" arguably have a better quality of life than the many unemployed black residents of Boston, their unwillingness to acknowledge the menial nature of their jobs while they look down at poorer blacks makes them just as snobbish as racist whites. As a bright youth who does not tolerate false pride or self-deception, Malcolm holds the overly judgmental habits of his middle-class neighbors in contempt.

Malcolm's experience shows that the tendency to deceive oneself is not tied to having money or being of a higher class than others.

The conk hairstyle, popular in middle-class and poor neighborhoods alike, represents black self-defacement and loss of identity. The act of conking, which physically forces black hair to resemble white hair, is representative of the way that black people attempt to imitate white society. "I know self-hatred first hand," claims Malcolm after describing in grim detail the process of straightening his own nappy hair with a powerful lye solution. Like the drinking and gambling in the ghetto and the pride and delusion of Roxbury Hill, Malcolm views the conk as yet another tactic blacks use to distract themselves from the real problems of their exploitation at the hands of white society. Malcolm sees blacks, unwilling to accept their true appearance, doing themselves physical harm in order to make their hair fit a white ideal of beauty. This need to mesh with white society plagues blacks of all classes because the cost of not fitting in to white society is often too great.

Malcolm uses his relationship with Sophia to escape the racial victimization of his youth by becoming a perpetrator of racism himself. Though Malcolm strongly criticizes the hypocrisy of his black neighbors, his relationship with Sophia makes him hypocritical in much the same way that his neighbors are. Malcolm's role reversal is an attempt to steal back the power that is earlier robbed from him in Michigan, where he is treated more like a pet than a human being. Although Malcolm has a serious romantic interest in his quiet black girlfriend, Laura, he leaves her for Sophia, an attractive white woman for whom he feels no love, in order to look good in front of his friends and acquaintances around Boston. Disrespecting Sophia's humanity is a way for Malcolm to enact revenge for the wrongs that white people have committed against him. His willingness to sacrifice his wholesome interest in Laura for his unwholesome abuse of Sophia represents the immaturity of his early attempts to combat racism.

Chapters Five, Six & Seven

Summary—Chapter Five: Harlemite

Malcolm finds a job washing dishes on a Boston–Washington train line and then selling sandwiches as a porter on a Boston–New York train line. He is dazzled by the wealth and energy of New York, especially Harlem's Savoy Ballroom and Apollo Theater. After being fired for taking the aggressive performances he uses to sell sandwiches too far, he is thrilled to work as a day waiter at a Harlem bar called Small's Paradise. Malcolm makes a good impression on the customers and on his employers, and learns various hustling techniques, the etiquette of the Harlem underworld, and the history of the neighborhood. With his tips, Malcolm begins to invest a lot of money in the numbers racket, the popular unofficial lottery in Harlem. He learns the names and faces of the young numbers runners as well as those of the "old heads," black gangsters left over from the 1920s and 1930s. Malcolm also meets an assortment of pimps, including one known as Sammy the Pimp, who soon becomes his best friend and sole Harlem confidant.

SUMMARY — CHAPTER SIX: DETROIT RED

> *All of us . . . were, instead, black victims of the white man's American social system.*
>
> *(See* QUOTATIONS, *p. 47)*

With permanent employment, Malcolm moves to a rooming house run by prostitutes. Malcolm befriends the women and learns a great deal about the psychology of men from them. Sophia, who has married a white man, visits Malcolm regularly. At first, she balks at Malcolm's living situation, but she soon befriends the prostitutes. Malcolm's friends begin calling him "Detroit Red" because his hair is bright red. After referring an undercover military agent to a prostitute, Malcolm loses his job and can no longer visit Small's. With the help of Sammy the Pimp, Malcolm begins to sell marijuana to New York's jazz musicians. At first, the business is a success, but soon the local narcotics squad comes after Malcolm, and he begins to lose time and money trying to avoid them. Eventually, Malcolm has to move weekly to avoid being arrested on planted evidence. He becomes addicted to the drugs he is supposed to be selling, and sometimes has to borrow money from Sammy just to eat. Sammy suggests that Malcolm use his old train-worker's identification to peddle marijuana up and down the East Coast.

SUMMARY — CHAPTER SEVEN: HUSTLER

Malcolm makes a trip to Boston, where Shorty is trying to get his band off the ground. During this visit, Malcolm's rendezvous with Sophia is more discreet than their previous encounters, partly because she is married and partly because World War II's toll on the United States' white population has increased popular fears about interracial romance. The draft board summons Malcolm. By dressing extravagantly and telling the army psychiatrist that he wishes to lead Southern blacks in murdering Southern whites, Malcolm evades the draft. The railroad company permanently blacklists Malcolm after he pulls a gun on a fellow gambler during a card game in the lower level of Grand Central Station in New York. The narcotics squad in Harlem knows Malcolm too well for him to resume his drug-dealing there, so he begins a series of robberies. Malcolm also begins trafficking guns and starts using harder drugs, primarily cocaine, to prepare for jobs and to deal with the stress they cause him.

When Malcolm's brother Reginald comes to stay with him in Harlem, Malcolm rents his first real apartment to ensure that he and his brother have a home. Malcolm also sets up Reginald with a hustle he claims is safe, in which Reginald pretends defective goods are stolen and sells them on the street for much more than what he pays. Conditions in Harlem begin worsening. The city government shuts down the Savoy Ballroom, and Harlem residents suspect that this measure is designed to stop single white women from dancing with black men. Two riots almost completely stop the flow of white tourists. Profits dry up for the nightlife industry, and hustlers and prostitutes begin to take on legitimate work. Malcolm has a falling out with Sammy the Pimp after Sammy pulls a gun on him for slapping one of Sammy's women. Eventually, Malcolm and Sammy make up, but they no longer fully trust each other. Malcolm begins to depend increasingly on Reginald, whom he describes as lazy but sensible.

ANALYSIS—CHAPTERS FIVE, SIX & SEVEN

Malcolm's firmly held belief that white people, and not black people, are to blame for the desperate conditions of the black underclass makes him lenient in his moral evaluation of the Harlem ghetto. Though Malcolm does blame some black people for their actions, most notably the middle-class, Civil Rights leaders, and himself, he tends to forgive residents of the black ghetto for their misdeeds and points instead to the conditions created by white society. In describing the Harlem ghetto, Malcolm blames his bosses in the numbers lottery system for draining the black ghetto of wealth. Whenever Malcolm describes the white pleasure-seekers that patronize the Harlem underworld of forbidden music, drugs, and women, he shows that these people make Harlem life harder by creating a demand for destructive activities like pimping and gambling, and by treating black people as objects. Though he does not spend much time making an explicit argument about moral responsibility, Malcolm's descriptions make it clear that he places the blame for the harshness of Harlem life on white New York and white America.

Malcolm believes that wealthy white people not only exploit poor blacks on a daily basis, but also contribute to the profound lack of opportunity in Harlem. In talking about the unrealized professional potential of his intelligent black friends, Malcolm implies that white society is to blame for driving them into the spiral of crime, drugs, deceit, and poverty, giving them no other option than the hustler's life. For instance, Sammy the Pimp's entrepreneurial drive might have made him a shrewd businessman, but in Harlem his skills are best suited for pimping, which eventually leads him to ruin. Later in the autobiography, Malcolm discusses his friend West Indian Archie's photographic memory and quick math skills, pointing out that these skills could have served him well in school, but Archie is instead locked into defending his gambling territory and his reputation, which eventually gets him killed. Even Malcolm's younger brother Reginald, a bright and gentle young man, needs to deceive his fellow Harlemites with a hustle in order to make ends meet. Malcolm's comparison of Harlem to a jungle in which only the fittest survive takes the weight of moral responsibility off of Harlem residents by showing that they are forced to engage in illegal and immoral acts by their harsh environment.

Although Malcolm strongly believes that white society is to blame for black America's problems, starting with slavery and continuing through segregation, his commentary in these chapters foreshadows his later belief that if blacks want a better life, it is up to them, and only them, to improve their situation. Malcolm's taking the blame for ruining Laura's life is an instance of the black community holding itself responsible for its failures. While Malcolm could easily blame white society and thereby ease his conscience and that of the black community in general, doing so would deny blacks power over lives such as Laura's. In blaming himself for Laura's downfall and thereby accepting responsibility for it, Malcolm shows his belief that he had the power to protect her from harmful influences. While Malcolm readily acknowledges that whites may be the source of such harmful influences, he feels it is necessary for other blacks to adopt a self-empowering attitude like his if they want to improve their lives.

Malcolm includes most of the details in these chapters to expose us to the tough side of the ghetto. However, the moments in which Malcolm portrays Harlem life in a positive light imply that there is an alternative to the white welfare state that offers to help the black people whom it simultaneously oppresses. Malcolm's feeling of kinship with the patrons of Small's Paradise shows that Harlem contains a network of people who are a source of community in a cruel world. Though money is tight, the black community prefers to help its own rather than receive assistance from a government institution, as with an elderly beggar named Fewclothes, whom the black community always given free meals. This presentation of an informal social safety net contrasts with the demeaning white welfare agencies that earlier divide Malcolm's family. In this instance, Malcolm shows that even people pushed to the brink of survival can form their own creative solutions to social problems.

CHAPTERS EIGHT & NINE

SUMMARY—CHAPTER EIGHT: TRAPPED

Malcolm takes on a variety of odd jobs in Harlem. For six months he transports betting slips for the numbers lottery system. Then, after working in a gambling parlor, Malcolm works for a madam, steering white people from downtown to the various places where their elaborate sexual fantasies can be fulfilled. In 1945 Malcolm is accused of robbing a craps game run by Italian racketeers. He begins to feel tense just walking the streets of Harlem. He quits his steering job and begins importing bootlegged liquor from Long Island for a Jewish businessman. He likes the work and his boss, but his boss disappears mysteriously after a scandal involving the bootlegging.

Malcolm himself plays the numbers more and more heavily, placing bets with West Indian Archie, an "old head" known for his photographic memory, which enables him not to have to write down any of the bets he takes. Malcolm hits a low point when West Indian Archie accuses him of collecting winnings on a bet he had not actually placed. Malcolm insists he has remembered correctly, and according to the code of the street, neither can back down. West Indian Archie gives Malcolm until the next day to return the money. Malcolm gets high on various drugs and wakes up long after the deadline. He returns to Harlem, where he runs into West Indian Archie at a bar. West Indian Archie humiliates Malcolm but does not shoot him, and a confrontation looms. The next day Malcolm punches a young hustler in the face, is almost stabbed, and is searched by the police. Now the cops, the Italian racketeers, the hustler Malcolm has just punched, and West Indian Archie are all out for Malcolm's blood, and he feels more threatened than ever. Just as Malcolm thinks he is going to get shot, Shorty picks him up and takes him to Boston.

SUMMARY—CHAPTER NINE: CAUGHT

In Boston, Shorty and Ella marvel at the transformed Malcolm, now edgy and foulmouthed from hustling. Malcolm takes a few weeks to unwind from the tension of his situation in Harlem, at first only sleeping, smoking marijuana, and playing records. Malcolm begins to do cocaine again and talks excessively to Shorty and Sophia about future plans. He remains close to Sophia, depending on her for money and marveling at how much abuse she takes. Sophia's husband is often on the road on business, which enables Malcolm to see a lot of Sophia. Shorty begins seeing Sophia's seventeen-year-old sister.

To make ends meet, Malcolm decides to find a new hustle. Using his reputation as ruthless and trigger-happy, he puts together a burglary ring consisting of himself, Shorty, and a local black Italian man named Rudy. They include Sophia and her sister to scope out white neighborhoods without arousing suspicion. Usually, the women visit a home as pollsters or salespeople and entice the housewife to give a tour. They then describe what they see in the house to the men, who go to the house at night. Shorty and Malcolm do the actual burglary, while Rudy mans the getaway car.

One day, while high on cocaine, Malcolm sees Sophia and her sister in a black bar with a white man who is a friend of Sophia's husband. Malcolm saunters over and addresses the women intimately, blowing Sophia's cover. The friend and then Sophia's husband himself later go on the hunt for him. When police arrest Malcolm in a pawn shop, he gives himself up peacefully. In court his conviction for stealing is due as much to his relationship with a white woman as it is to his burglary. Malcolm notes that the police cross-examine him on the origin and nature of his relationships with the women instead of on the crime of burglary with which he is charged. The judge sentences him to ten years in state prison.

ANALYSIS—CHAPTERS EIGHT & NINE

In these chapters, Malcolm shows us the depths to which he sinks in Harlem so that we can understand the dramatic nature of the education and conversion he subsequently undergoes in prison. His statement that "[a]ll of our experiences fuse into our personality" reflects his belief that he must understand his past to understand his present. Malcolm's education allows him to reevaluate the forms of racism he experienced earlier in his life. Whereas before his time in prison he responds to individual encounters of prejudice as separate instances of personal attacks, his new, more fully developed perspective on race relations leads him to see them as part of a single problem. His conversion to Islam similarly leads him to a more expanded understanding of racial problems. He now understands them on both a national and international level: white America has mistreated black America from slavery through segregation, and Western societies have historically used and abused nonwhites. Just as his conversion to Islam offers him the possibility of redemption under Allah, his process of self-discovery offers him the possibility of a more productive, though still limited, place in society.

The changes in Malcolm's philosophies about race connect directly to his changing understanding of racism. Throughout his youth Malcolm sees himself primarily as a victim of unfair discrimination: white society murders his father, divides his family, treats him as inferior, and discourages him from success. He interprets this racism as a direct attack on him personally rather than as an attack on his race. As Malcolm develops his understanding of race relations in prison, however, he interprets his early experience of racism in the context of American history and society. He begins to see black people in general, rather than just himself, as victims of racism. Malcolm now understands that the lifestyles and goals of his peers in Roxbury Hill and Harlem and the jobs and schools available to them are heavily influenced by his peers' inhabiting the slums of a white city. With this realization, Malcolm comes to view racism not as a personal attack on an individual but as a blind attack on blackness in general. This changing attitude toward racism influences his later espousal of anti–white rhetoric and militant black separatism.

Malcolm's conversion to Islam allows him to interpret his years of crime as an experience that, while negative, is necessary for personal growth. After Malcolm converts to Islam, he views these years as a descent to the bottom of white society that prepares him to accept the religion's cleansing message. The cleansing message of the religion has a powerful impact on him because he has led such a sinful life. Though Malcolm admits the destructive nature of his wild youth and condemns the activities in which he engaged, he is nonetheless unashamed of having been a ruthless, violent criminal. He believes that the will of Allah has brought him to the righteous path by first putting him through suffering and sin. Islam simulta-

neously humbles and affirms Malcolm; as by showing him the error
of his ways it also shows him the path to redemption.

CHAPTERS TEN & ELEVEN

SUMMARY—CHAPTER TEN: SATAN

Malcolm's time in Massachusetts state prison is a period of intellectual growth and religious upheaval. Suffering from drug with-
drawal and a fierce temper, he is placed in solitary confinement and
nicknamed "Satan." He meets Bimbi, a confident black prisoner
whose speech commands the respect of guards and inmates alike.
Under Bimbi's instruction, Malcolm begins to think outside the hustler mindset of his youth. He makes use of the small prison library,
refines his English, and channels his rage into reasoned argument. In
1948 Malcolm moves to Norfolk Prison Colony, where there is less
violence and inmates may study and debate freely. At the huge
library there, he immerses himself in subject after subject, including
history, religion, literature, biology, and linguistics.

Malcolm first hears about the Nation of Islam from his family.
He gives up pork at his brother Reginald's request, later seeing this
decision as his first step toward becoming a Muslim. Reginald tells
him about the Nation of Islam's spiritual leader, Elijah Muhammad,
whose central teaching is that all white men are devils. While decid-
ing whether to convert, Malcolm thinks of all the white people he
has ever known. He remembers the social workers who split up his
family, the teacher who discouraged him from becoming a lawyer,
and his customers when he worked as a porter and a pimp. He also
considers the white policemen, judge, and guards who have conspired to lock him away. Every one of these people, he reflects, has
done him harm. He begins to undergo an overwhelming change and
to feel that the sin and guilt of his past have prepared him to accept
the truth of Islam.

Malcolm accepts the Nation of Islam's principles. According to
Elijah Muhammad, the first humans were black, living peacefully
under Allah in Mecca. Then, a mad scientist named Mr. Yacub
unleashed an evil race of white people on Europe who conspired to
abuse nonwhites for 6,000 years. Elijah Muhammad teaches that
black people were stolen from Africa, sold into bondage, and finally
brainwashed. White people forced them to adopt the names, customs, myths, and god of their masters. Now, however, white civili-

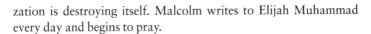

zation is destroying itself. Malcolm writes to Elijah Muhammad every day and begins to pray.

SUMMARY—CHAPTER ELEVEN: SAVED

To improve his writing skills, Malcolm slowly copies out the whole dictionary longhand, starting with the word *"aardvark."* With an expanded vocabulary, he begins to read voraciously, staying up half the night to study in his cell. He says that reading awakens his "long dormant craving to be mentally alive." Malcolm soon develops a system of beliefs that has Africa at its center. From reputable sources he learns that the first men and the great early civilizations were African, that the pharaohs were Africans, and that the great Western storyteller Aesop was an African. The horror of slavery and the bold nineteenth-century revolts of Nat Turner and John Brown impact him deeply. Studying the anti-British resistance of India and China, he also discovers that colonial exploitation, and opposition to it, was not limited to Africa.

The prison's debate program introduces Malcolm to public speaking. He almost always finds a way to work the idea of race into his arguments, whether they are about military service or Shakespeare. Debate teaches him rhetorical skills he later uses to earn converts to the Nation of Islam. He is thrilled by his success in making a white minister publicly admit that Jesus was not white. He resolves to devote the rest of his life to telling the white man about himself or to die trying. Soon, Reginald is suspended from the Nation of Islam for sleeping with a secretary. After Elijah Muhammad appears to Malcolm in a silent vision, Malcolm disowns Reginald and for the first time feels a stronger bond to his faith than to his family. Reginald goes insane, and Malcolm comes to believe that Allah is punishing Reginald for his sins. Malcolm continues to seek converts to Islam among his fellow prisoners.

ANALYSIS—CHAPTERS TEN & ELEVEN

The language that Malcolm uses in telling his story shows how his perspective has changed since the time of the events that he describes. The younger Malcolm views his life in terms of absolute good and evil. Accordingly, he uses strongly opposing terms, such as "white" and "black" and "good" and "bad," in his descriptions. He sees the world according to these rigid pairs, and thus too simply. The language he uses to interpret his life contains only these sorts of absolute terms, and he ignores the parts of his previous life that do

SUMMARY & ANALYSIS

not' fit with the principles he has accepted from Elijah Muhammad. For example, he has known many white people, including his foster parents, his Jewish former boss, and his lover Sophia, who have treated him decently. But because Malcolm longs for moral clarity, he associates all that is good, original, and pure with the term "black" and all that is evil, derivative, and tainted with the term "white." While it is necessary for Malcolm to combat racist stereotypes of blacks, the manner in which he does so is problematic, because it leads to racist stereotypes of whites. In reversing the racist association of white with good and black with bad, Malcolm does not help alleviate racism but rather stirs it up in a different direction.

The voice that Malcolm uses in telling the story of his youth, on the other hand, shows that he has developed a more complex view of good and evil as an adult. His mention of "the entire spectrum of white people I had ever known" illustrates his more mature understanding of his early experiences. The word "spectrum" denotes a range of things, such as colors, that differ from each other in varying degrees. Malcolm's use of this word shows that he has by now abandoned his earlier, simplistic view of the world. He no longer thinks of people as strictly white, and thus bad, or strictly black, and thus good. He has recognized that within the category of "white" there is a whole spectrum of individual human personalities to judge. He is able to see that some white people may be bad, while others may be good, just as some black people may be good, while others may be bad. In choosing the word "spectrum," the older and wiser Malcolm conveys his understanding that his early attitudes toward race were not consistent with his early life experience.

The anti–white prejudice that Malcolm adopts upon converting to the Nation of Islam differed from much twentieth-century American prejudice. Unlike prejudices against various ethnic, racial, or political minorities, anti–white prejudice was not the social norm. Since the end of slavery, whites had accused blacks of taking their jobs, corrupting their schools, and degrading their neighborhoods. Whites' fear of blacks was a major factor in the creation of racist laws and segregation. Similarly, after the bombing of Pearl Harbor in 1941, many Americans became very suspicious of people of Japanese descent and confined them to internment camps. Finally, in the 1950s, widespread paranoia about suspected communists produced a rash of trials and executions known as McCarthyism. However, Elijah Muhammad's rhetoric of "blue-eyed devils" and "original people" is different from prejudice against blacks, Japanese, and suspected communists. The Nation of Islam was the movement of a separatist minority with a very small following. In contrast, racism against blacks, anti-Japanese hysteria, and McCarthyism were mainstream movements attracting millions of Americans and encompassing many institutions, both private and public.

CHAPTERS TWELVE & THIRTEEN

SUMMARY — CHAPTER TWELVE: SAVIOR

> *Yes! Yes, that raping, red-headed devil was my*
> *grandfather! . . . . I hate every drop of the rapist's blood*
> *that's in me!*
>
> *(See* QUOTATIONS, *p. 48)*

In August 1952, the prison releases Malcolm on parole into the custody of his brother Wilfred. Malcolm buys a wristwatch, a suitcase, and a pair of eyeglasses. In Detroit, Malcolm instantly appreciates the warmth and order of Wilfred's strictly Muslim household. The solidarity and austerity of his first Nation of Islam temple meeting excites Malcolm. In Chicago Elijah Muhammad publicly likens Malcolm to the biblical figure Job, inviting everyone to watch the strength of Malcolm's faith now that the safety of prison is gone and he is back out among the temptations of the real world. At dinner that night, Malcolm asks Elijah Muhammad about recruitment techniques, as he is eager to work to attract new members in Detroit. Elijah Muhammad advises Malcolm to court young people.

In Detroit Malcolm has little luck at first, persuading only a few neighborhood youth to visit the temple. Over several months, however, membership triples. During this period, Malcolm replaces his last name with "X" to represent the unknown African name he would have had if his ancestors not been kidnapped and enslaved. Malcolm begins to speak at temple meetings and gains confidence as an orator. He is surprised, humbled, and flattered when Elijah Muhammad appoints him as the assistant minister at the Detroit temple.

Malcolm soon learns Elijah Muhammad's life story. Born in Georgia in 1897, Elijah Muhammad was small of stature but bold, especially when it came to issues of race. He mediated fights between his siblings and was frank but nonconfrontational with white employers. In 1931, in Detroit, Elijah Muhammad met Wallace D. Fard, a peddler and self-proclaimed prophet who converted him to his version of Islam. By the time Fard disappeared in 1934,

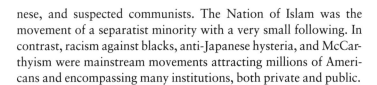

Elijah Muhammad was at the helm of the Nation of Islam. Death threats from jealous rivals, however, compelled Elijah Muhammad to move himself and his family from city to city for seven years. He spent time in prison, supposedly for draft evasion, although he was in fact too old to serve in the military. Only in the 1940s did he reclaim his position as the head of the Nation of Islam.

SUMMARY — CHAPTER THIRTEEN: MINISTER MALCOLM X

Elijah Muhammad needs ministers for his growing nation, so Malcolm X quits his job at the Ford Motor Company and begins extensive training. During this time, Malcolm fully develops his rhetorical style. When Malcolm is ready, Elijah Muhammad sends him to Boston to aid in the founding of a temple there. Malcolm visits his old haunts and tries to convert Shorty, who loves white women and pork too much to be persuaded. Ella is amazed at Malcolm, and although she does not convert, she is happy to see he has changed. Once the Boston temple is up and running, Elijah Muhammad sends Malcolm to Philadelphia. Early in the summer of 1954, Muhammad appoints Malcolm to found the small New York Temple. As in Boston, Malcolm seeks out his old crowd. He discovers that Sammy the Pimp is dead and that West Indian Archie is dying. The lack of response to his initial teachings frustrates Malcolm, but he continues, and the temple grows. Malcolm and his followers develop techniques for drawing blacks from black nationalist rallies and churches that advocate a return to Africa. Malcolm has so much luck winning over Christians that he refines his speaking style with them in mind, emphasizing Christianity's role in the oppression of blacks.

In 1956 a woman named Betty joins the New York temple. For ten years, Malcolm has been celibate and fully devoted to his work. He hardly courts Betty, but he approves of her from a distance. Malcolm introduces Betty to Elijah Muhammad, and then proposes marriage abruptly from a payphone in Detroit. They marry and settle in Queens, New York, and have four children while Malcolm is alive; a fifth child is born after Malcolm's death.

In 1958, Malcolm's half-sister, Ella, converts to the Nation of Islam. The Nation of Islam gets public recognition when police attack one of its members. The "Fruit of Islam," the Nation's elite youth group, leads a mass demonstration, standing ominously before the precinct house where the bleeding victim is being held and then before the hospital to which Malcolm has demanded the victim be taken. Later, the Nation of Islam wins $70,000 in a lawsuit against the city. Malcolm is so busy that the Nation buys him a car to use for his travel between cities. Having taken a vow of poverty, Malcolm has access to the Nation's substantial resources but personally owns almost nothing. By 1965, there are sizable temples in Chicago, Detroit, and New York.

ANALYSIS—CHAPTERS TWELVE & THIRTEEN

Malcolm's purchase of a wristwatch, suitcase, and eyeglasses upon leaving Massachusetts state prison symbolizes his newfound time-conscious efficiency, tireless drive, and mature vision. If Malcolm's earlier peaceful surrender to the Boston detective marks the beginning of his prison conversion, then the purchase of these amenities marks the completion of this same conversion as well as the beginning of his career of religious and political authority. Whereas his initial surrender to the detectives is a passive act of submission, this purchase is an active act of self-possession. Malcolm's statement that "without fully knowing it, I was preparing for what my life was about to become" shows his instinctive determination. In picking up the tools of his trade as soon as he is released from prison, Malcolm makes a symbolic commitment to a life of authority and responsibility with the Nation of Islam and beyond.

The wristwatch, suitcase, and eyeglasses each symbolize an important aspect of Malcolm's career as a Muslim minister and political figure. The wristwatch represents his obsession with efficiently managing his busy daily schedule. He is committed to the people and events of his daily life, not distanced from them as Elijah Muhammad and other religious leaders are. The suitcase represents Malcolm's commitment to a life of constant work and frequent travel in the name of spreading Islam. His travel allows him to interact with other blacks nationwide and other minorities worldwide, and such experiences help him develop a more mature perspective on the struggle against oppression. Malcolm's eyeglasses represent his newfound clarity of vision on race in America. Though the glasses serve the practical purpose of correcting the vision problems Malcolm has developed from years of reading in prison, they also serve the symbolic purpose of correcting his understanding of the issues at hand. His statement that "in all my years in the streets, I'd been looking at the exploitation that for the first time I really saw and understood" shows that his time in prison has made him see the race problem clearly. With his commitment to his message, connection to his people, and understanding of the problems plaguing his people, Malcolm is prepared to launch himself into a new and productive life.

In Chapter 12, "Savior," both Malcolm and Elijah Muhammad compare Malcolm's faith in Islam to Job's faith in God, each using the biblical parable to make a different point. As the story goes, Satan challenged God to test Job's faith by making him suffer through various trials. While Elijah Muhammad uses the story to highlight Malcolm's ability to resist the temptations of his former life once released from prison, Malcolm uses the story to draw attention to the trial of his faith that his difficult relationship with Elijah Muhammad creates. Though these comparisons serve different purposes, both point out Malcolm's ability to stand behind his ideological convictions and carry on a prolonged struggle against difficult odds.

Malcolm's discussion of his relationship with Elijah Muhammad reveals that he sees Elijah Muhammad more as a god than as a human. Elijah Muhammad's assertion that Malcolm will remain a faithful Muslim out of prison reciprocates and intensifies Malcolm's faith in Elijah Muhammad. Elijah Muhammad's confidence inspires years of near-absolute devotion from Malcolm, and Malcolm describes having more faith in Elijah Muhammad than in any other man. Malcolm foreshadows how this great faith in Elijah actually proves the downfall of their relationship with his statement that "I know today that I did believe in him more firmly than he believed in himself." This quote implies that Allah's greatest trial for Malcolm is Elijah Muhammad himself. Although Elijah Muhammad inspires Malcolm to persist in the face of adversity, his own faltering in the face of adversity later becomes an obstacle in their relationship.

CHAPTERS FOURTEEN, FIFTEEN & SIXTEEN

SUMMARY — CHAPTER FOURTEEN: BLACK MUSLIMS

In 1957, after visiting the black-run *Herald Dispatch* in Los Angeles, Malcolm founds *Muhammad Speaks,* the Nation of Islam's own newspaper. A surge of publicity comes in 1959, when a man named C. Eric Lincoln publishes a book called *The Black Muslims in America* and a program on the Nation called *The Hate that Hate Produced* airs on television. Both titles enrage Malcolm, who realizes that the media will spin everything for shock value. Soon, mainstream publications, including *Life* and *Time,* feature articles about the Nation of Islam. Malcolm now spends hours a day on the tele-

SUMMARY & ANALYSIS

phone defending the Nation and attacking his interviewers with countercharges, clarifications, and assertions of bias. Increasingly, organizations invite Malcolm to represent Elijah Muhammad on panels and lecture circuits.

In the fall of 1959, Malcolm travels as an emissary to places where leaders are becoming interested in the Nation of Islam project: Egypt, Arabia, Sudan, Nigeria, and Ghana. Exposed to more radical ideas, he becomes increasingly critical of black civil rights leaders, calling them "integration-mad Negroes" and "Uncle Toms." At first, Elijah Muhammad discourages any disparagement of other black leaders, but when attacks on the Nation become too frequent, he lets Malcolm vent his feelings publicly. By 1960, the Nation of Islam starts holding mass rallies with Elijah Muhammad as the main attraction. At first the Nation admits no white people to these rallies, but eventually they admit the white press and then anyone with curiosity.

The size and militance of the Nation attracts the attention of the FBI and the police, who begin infiltrating rallies and tapping the telephones of higher-ups, including Malcolm X. Part of this government interest comes from the high proportion of Nation of Islam members who are or were in prison. Convicts embrace the Nation because their prison experiences have conditioned them both to take an especially grim view of white society and to excel at the discipline and austerity that the codes of the Nation demand. The Nation also succeeds in reforming drug addicts.

SUMMARY—CHAPTER FIFTEEN: ICARUS
On the recommendation of the aging Elijah Muhammad's doctors, the Nation buys Elijah Muhammad a home in Arizona, where he begins to spend most of the year. Elijah Muhammad's geographical distance and diminished health, as well as the growing administrative demands of the Nation, lead Malcolm to make a greater number of decisions without notifying Muhammad. By 1963 both the Nation of Islam and Malcolm X are inundated with publicity. Now the second most sought-after university lecturer in America, Malcolm X savors the excitement of the intellectual confrontations that follow his speeches at top universities. Elijah Muhammad disapproves of the university lecture circuit, while other Muslims frequently accuse Malcolm of trying to take over the Nation of Islam. Malcolm notices that his name is appearing less and less in *Muhammad Speaks,* the newspaper he himself founded. He begins turning

SUMMARY & ANALYSIS

down publicity opportunities in *Life* and *Newsweek*, hoping to reduce Elijah Muhammad's jealousy.

Summary — Chapter Sixteen: Out

Malcolm's relationship to the Nation of Islam becomes more complex when Elijah Muhammad faces paternity suits from two temple secretaries. At first, Malcolm pretends that he does not know about the allegations and changes his temple teachings to skirt the issue of the moral code. Eventually, however, he approaches Elijah Muhammad for advice. Elijah Muhammad compares himself to the great men of scripture whose accomplishments outweigh their occasional transgressions. Malcolm accepts this explanation and assumes that Elijah Muhammad will confess and explain himself to the Nation. Elijah Muhammad does not publicly confess, however.

Relations worsen between Malcolm and the Nation of Islam after President John F. Kennedy is assassinated. Malcolm breaks an order by Elijah Muhammad that no minister comment on the assassination. He calls the murder in Dallas a case of "the chickens coming home to roost," a statement that implies that the murder was somehow justifiable. To distance the Nation from such a controversial stance, Elijah Muhammad silences Malcolm for a ninety-day period. Malcolm soon realizes, however, that Elijah Muhammad's outrage over the Kennedy quote is merely an excuse for the Nation to cast him off, as it has been plotting to do for some time. Malcolm is deeply shocked at Elijah Muhammad's betrayal of him, describing it as a sudden divorce after twelve years of beautiful marriage.

Malcolm hears rumors of a warrant out for his death, and one of his assistants at the New York temple confesses that the Nation has ordered him to kill Malcolm. To distance himself from the Nation of Islam and absorb the shock of the symbolic divorce, Malcolm accepts the invitation of boxer Cassius Clay for Malcolm and his family to stay in Florida while Clay prepares for his fight against Sonny Liston. The sight of Clay, who has Islamic leanings, defeating a fighter who is physically stronger through a combination of will, cleverness, and training strengthens Malcolm's faith in Allah. Clay announces his Muslim affiliation after the fight, taking the name "Muhammad Ali."

Once Malcolm accepts his estrangement from the Nation of Islam, he thinks about how he can continue to serve the political and economic interests of black people. He decides to use his celebrity status to found an organization called "Muslim

Mosque, Inc." in Harlem. Malcolm envisions the organization as more inclusive and more active than the Nation of Islam in its pursuit of black political and economic independence. Before things really get going, however, Malcolm decides that it is time for him to make his pilgrimage to the Islamic holy city of Mecca. Cut off from his sole source of income, the Nation, Malcolm asks Ella for money for the trip, and she obliges.

ANALYSIS — CHAPTERS FOURTEEN, FIFTEEN & SIXTEEN

Malcolm makes use of what he learns early in life as a hustler to gain and maintain prominence in the Nation of Islam. While he does not condone the hustler's life, his comments imply a respect for the hustler's code of ethics. The street rules—"be suspicious," "know your enemy," and "image is everything"—are as well suited to Malcolm's outspoken public life as to his petty hustling life. By never trusting anyone outside his close circle of friends, Malcolm keeps the growing network of mosques across America under his direct control as he expands the reach of the Nation of Islam. His occasional failure to follow these rules illustrates how important they are. Malcolm puts his faith in Elijah Muhammad after the scandal breaks that Elijah Muhammad slept with his secretaries, and Elijah Muhammad repays Malcolm by silencing him, exiling him, and repeatedly trying to have him killed. When Malcolm trusts Elijah Muhammad too much and thereby breaks one of the hustler's rules, he experiences grave consequences.

Like a hustler, Malcolm tries to understand his enemy's psychology in order to guard against danger and tries to develop a strong public image to inspire fear. As Malcolm deals with the resistance of the police and the white press to his political activities, he never loses sight of the necessity of knowing how they work in order to be able to challenge them effectively. For instance, after visiting a Los Angeles newspaper for a week, Malcolm becomes ready to launch an informed counterattack, in the form of his own Muslim newspaper, *Muhammad Speaks*. Furthermore, as an activist Malcolm carefully shapes his public image, just as he does earlier as a hustler. While his obsession with defending his image leads Malcolm to near-death in a duel with West Indian Archie, it allows him to deal effectively with the white press. Not afraid to ignore questions or answer questions that are different from the ones the press poses him, Malcolm uses his smooth-talking skill to fine-tune his public image to his advantage. His understanding of the similarity between hustling individuals and hustling the public enables him to stay out of the way, temporarily, of the dangerous intentions that his ideas provoke.

The skills Malcolm acquires as a hustler in Harlem also help him turn his ambitions for the expansion of the Nation of Islam into a reality. As Malcolm rapidly rises through the Nation's ranks, a religious fervor for recruitment drives him, and he eventually crosses the country to found temples in Boston, Harlem, Detroit, Philadelphia, and Los Angeles. His experience as a quick judge of character helps him run the new temples smoothly, and his knowledge of street psychology and slang makes him more persuasive than his Christian competitors to many young black city-dwellers. Still, with all his credibility, he finds the majority unreachable, plagued by social, spiritual, economic, and political problems. The most important part of Malcolm's Harlem experience is the knowledge that blacks must be aggressive about helping themselves if they want to improve their situation.

Although Malcolm and Elijah Muhammad both fight for black rights, they differ in their estimation of how the struggle for these rights should be carried out. While Elijah Muhammad wants American blacks to adopt an Asian identity and speak Arabic, Malcolm continues to believe in a version of his father's pan-Africanism, inspired by Marcus Garvey. While Elijah Muhammad wants American blacks to be their own kind of middle-class Americans in conservative suits, Malcolm remains more interested in the plight of the poor. Both men agree that the correct response to segregation is not integration but cultural and economic separation. However, they could not disagree more on how to achieve these goals: while Elijah Muhammad wants to keep his organization wholly apart from politics, Malcolm often wants to be engaged in action for racial justice. That there are such differences of opinion between two leaders within the same group illustrates the complexity of the race issue in America.

Chapters Seventeen, Eighteen & Nineteen

Summary — Chapter Seventeen: Mecca

America needs to understand Islam, because this is the one religion that erases from its society the race problem.

(*See* Quotations, *p. 49*)

Malcolm explains that every Muslim must, if possible, make a pilgrimage, or hajj, to the holy city of Mecca in Saudi Arabia. Malcolm has no trouble receiving financial backing from Ella, who has also withdrawn from the Nation of Islam. When Malcolm applies for a hajj visa, he learns that his status as a Muslim must be approved by Mahmoud Youssef Shawarbi, a Muslim United Nations advisor.

Malcolm leaves the United States and goes to see sights in Cairo. He then flies to Jedda, Saudi Arabia, where officials confiscate his passport and tell him a high court must establish whether or not he is a true Muslim. Officials send him to a crowded airport dormitory, where he reflects on the various languages, colors, and customs of the Muslims around him. Malcolm calls Omar Azzam, a friend of Shawarbi's, for help. Azzam vacates his father's suite at the Jedda Palace Hotel for Malcolm. This hospitality impresses Malcolm, who enjoys fine food and conversation with Jedda's elite and is lent a car by Saudi Arabia's Prince Faisal himself to make the hajj to Mecca.

Malcolm describes his sense of wonder at Mecca. During his visit, he admires the Islamic world's lack of racial divisions. At the end of the hajj, Malcolm writes letters home that express his changed perspective on racial problems in the United States. Having met white-skinned people who are untainted by racism, Malcolm now locates America's problems in the white attitude generated by four hundred years of collective violence against blacks. He sees Islam as a solution to America's problems. Malcolm signs all of his letters "El-Hajj Malik El-Shabazz," which becomes his official name, although the world continues to refer to him as Malcolm X.

SUMMARY — CHAPTER EIGHTEEN: "EL-HAJJ MALIK EL-SHABAZZ"

The American Negro has been entirely brainwashed from ever seeing or thinking of himself, as he should, as a part of the nonwhite peoples of the world.

(See QUOTATIONS, *p. 50)*

Malcolm learns that leaders and intellectuals of nonwhite nations are interested in the plight of American blacks. Malcolm flies to Lebanon, where he is warmly received. In Ghana, a high commissioner gives Malcolm ceremonial robes. Malcolm then visits Liberia, Senegal, and Morocco before returning home. In New York, reporters besiege him with questions that imply a connection between him and race riots erupting across the country. The press's failure to acknowledge Malcolm's new outlook frustrates him.

SUMMARY — CHAPTER NINETEEN: "1965"

I'm for truth, no matter who tells it. I'm for justice, no matter who it is for or against.

(See QUOTATIONS, *p. 51)*

In Harlem Malcolm holds meetings for a new organization, the Organization for Afro-American Unity. He emphasizes its inclusiveness of people of any faith, though it excludes whites from membership. Malcolm believes that whites should change their own communities in separate organizations and that black people must unify before they band together with whites to fight racism. Malcolm returns to Africa and the Middle East for another eighteen weeks, meeting with many world leaders. He confesses to feeling stifled in his new endeavors by his reputation. He predicts that he will die a violent death, doubting that he will live to see the publication of his autobiography.

ANALYSIS — CHAPTERS SEVENTEEN, EIGHTEEN & NINETEEN

Malcolm's articulation of a new vision for black Americans, urging them to see themselves as one of a number of nonwhite minorities seeking justice worldwide, shows how his openness to new experiences allows him to develop philosophies that greatly contrast with those he espoused previously. His visits to several African nations that have recently won their independence from European colonial powers, as well as to socialist Egypt and anti-imperialist India, inspire his vision of a worldwide context for the civil rights movement. Instead of resisting the differences between their version of Islam and his own, he thoughtfully considers how their philosophy can be applied to blacks in America. Malcolm's intention to bring the United States in front of a U.N. tribunal on the charges of mass human rights violations demonstrates the extent of his commitment to a new kind of Islam.

Though Malcolm first espouses a worldwide view of racial oppression in this chapter, earlier sections of the autobiography hint that Malcolm will eventually relate the struggle of blacks in America to the struggles of other oppressed groups. For example, while describing his first impressions of New York City in Chapter Five, "Harlemite," Malcolm traces the history of the Harlem ghetto as a place where minority racial groups have confined themselves. In seeing blacks as part of a series of American immigrant groups' struggle to escape the ghetto, Malcolm relates racism against blacks to bias against Germans, Italians, Jews, and the Dutch. But Malcolm feels that prejudice against blacks, while similar to the prejudices against these other groups, is more deep-rooted and more difficult to remedy. He aligns the struggle of American blacks with the struggle of minorities in other countries because he believes that the political and economical problems of American blacks are more similar to the problems of blacks in other parts of the world than to those of other groups in America. Though ethnic minorities in America have had to fight prejudice, they have not suffered the same degree of oppression and subjugation as the many black peoples whom whites reduced to slavery.

The great change that Malcolm undergoes at the end of the autobiography parallels the change that he earlier undergoes in prison. In both cases, he abandons his radical views on race and broadens his perspective. His time in prison, during which he educates himself and converts to Islam, shows him the need to bring the struggle for equality to the black masses. After his release from prison, he no longer wants to get by for himself; rather, he wants blacks to unify and fight for their due as a people. Similarly, his time in the Middle East exposes him to new points of view and offers him new insight into how to resolve racial tensions. For example, during his pilgrimage to Mecca and his subsequent stops in the Middle East, Malcolm witnesses the "colorblindness" of the Islamic world. This colorblindness refers to a model of racial integration that Malcolm actively resists earlier. Seeing its effectiveness in another environment, however, changes Malcolm's attitude toward it. He emerges from his travels convinced that oppressed nonwhite groups throughout the world must unite to eliminate white oppression altogether. In both cases, Malcolm's openness to the wisdom around him helps him develop a more mature outlook. His constant growth as a person shows that he is not a mere angry revolutionary who wants vengeance against whites but a leader sincerely interested in achieving racial harmony.

Epilogue

Summary

NOTE: *The epilogue differs from the other chapters of the autobiography in that it is told from Alex Haley's point of view.*

Alex Haley first hears about the Nation of Islam while in San Francisco in 1959 and first meets Malcolm X in New York in 1960. He writes two articles on Malcolm X and one on Elijah Muhammad before a publisher proposes to Haley the idea of a biography. Having won the trust of Malcolm and Elijah Muhammad with the earlier pieces, Haley gets them both to agree to the project.

Haley gains Malcolm X's trust over a long period of interviews. Malcolm, who suspects all reporters, including black ones, of serving white America, is at first very cautious about Haley's project. After almost giving up because Malcolm refuses to produce anything but Nation of Islam rhetoric, Haley observes that Malcolm often scribbles on scraps of paper around him with a red pen. Haley then starts laying out note cards before each interview and collecting them afterward with Malcolm's scribblings on them. These fragments of Malcolm's private thoughts prove instrumental for Haley in understanding Malcolm.

Slowly, after numerous interview sessions with Haley in New York City, Malcolm opens up. Haley begins work on the autobiography shortly before Malcolm's falling out with Elijah Muhammad, and the epilogue traces the last two years of Malcolm's life from Haley's point of view. Haley emphasizes the tension and violence surrounding Malcolm's final days and describes in detail the death threats that precede Malcolm's assassination.

On February 21, 1965, three audience members at a lecture at Harlem's Audubon Ballroom, which Malcolm has been renting to use for his new organization, shoot and kill Malcolm X. Police arrest three suspects, all with Muslim affiliations, who are later convicted. However, comments that Malcolm made in his final days suggest that somebody more powerful than the Nation of Islam may have had a hand in the killing. Haley describes Malcolm's funeral, which is attended by thousands of blacks, whites, Muslims, and non-Muslims. The funeral rites are performed by, among others, a sheikh, or Arab man, from Mecca. The sheikh ends with a description of the Islamic view of life after the Day of Judgment, thereby hinting that Malcolm has ascended to paradise.

ANALYSIS

The epilogue raises the question of whether or not *The Autobiography of Malcolm X* is more autobiography or biography. In describing his unusual collaboration with Malcolm X, Alex Haley shows that the work is a product of both of their minds. Though Haley is one of the most famous African-American nonfiction authors of the twentieth century, questions have arisen about his scholarly integrity. Some critics have dismissed his later work, *Roots,* in which Haley attempts to trace the generations of his own family from Africa to the present day, as poorly researched. Although *The Autobiography of Malcolm X* involves much more straightforward research, and Malcolm X did approve most of the text before his death, some critics nevertheless lament that the autobiography's voice appears to be as much Haley's as Malcolm's. They fear that the collaborative nature of the work may have stifled Malcolm, who was as eager to teach others as he was to learn.

The slips of paper on which Malcolm scribbles unconsciously at each interview reveal that Malcolm maintained an independent and open-minded current of thought, free of the rhetoric that he publicly embraced and propagated. The first slip of paper Haley recovers, written at the peak of Malcolm's submission to Elijah Muhammad, reveals a fiercely independent mind reaching out to understand hate in another context. Its musing that "[i]f Christianity had asserted itself in Germany six million Jews would have lived" reflects a religious tolerance that was unacceptable by the Nation of Islam's standards. Despite his commitment to the Nation's goals, Malcolm broadened his concern beyond prejudice against blacks to prejudice against all people. The next scribbling, recovered by Haley in the tumultuous period of the break with Elijah Muhammad, further underscores Malcolm's dedication to his true beliefs even when they went against the Nation's. Its statement that "you have not converted a man because you have silenced him" resonates with both its immediate and general circumstances. The immediate circumstance was Elijah Muhammad's silencing of Malcolm after Malcolm made unpopular remarks about President Kennedy's assassination. While the Nation of Islam remained respectful to the slain leader, Malcolm viewed the assassination as the logical outcome of U.S. social turmoil. The general circumstance surrounding this quote was that while Malcolm had been censoring himself and deferring to the word of Elijah Muhammad for a long time, he never truly subjugated his principles.

Malcolm's comment, made during his conversion to a more tolerant vision of Islam, that "my life has always been one of changes" alludes to his lifelong trajectory toward global tolerance. Though simple, this observation points to Malcolm's openness to change, which in turn points to the sincerity of his quest to resolve the race issues that have always surrounded him. When, as Malcolm Little, he can no longer tolerate being treated as a pet, Malcolm leaves for the big city to explore his black identity. As Detroit Red he becomes notorious with musicians, gamblers, and hustlers in Boston and Harlem, but he eventually gives himself up after recognizing the emptiness of this fast lifestyle. In prison, Malcolm matures from a vicious inmate known as "Satan" into a voracious intellectual. He emerges as Malcolm X and, committed to getting people politically active, extends the Nation of Islam across the United States. Late in his life, as El-Hajj Malik El-Shabazz, Malcolm focuses on developing a global unity between oppressed peoples, finally convinced that a cooperative effort on the part of many groups can improve the lot of blacks everywhere. The lengthy and varied trajectory of his path shows that the poor race relations between blacks and whites in the United States constitute a complex problem with no easy solution.

SUMMARY & ANALYSIS

Important Quotations Explained

1. In one sense, we were huddled in there, bonded togethher in seeking security and warmth and comfort from each other, and we didn't know it. All of us—who might have probed space, or cured cancer, or built industries—were, instead, black victims of the white man's American social system.

This passage from Chapter Six, "Detroit Red," describes the Harlem nightclub as a family network and a safe space that counterbalances the overwhelming forces of racism in the outside world. The description is typical of the autobiography in its portrayal of members of the Harlem community as victims of racial oppression. Faced with this political reality, those who frequent these nightclubs must concern themselves mainly with the basic matter of surviving the conditions of the ghetto. The nightclubs have become something of a home for these blacks. Malcolm's assertion that the nightclub regulars use this family network without knowing it underscores how vital this support is to their survival. Many of the regulars are poised, aggressive hustlers on the outside, but their need for "security and warmth and comfort" persists on the inside.

This passage also focuses on the wasted potential of the black masses. It refers indirectly to Malcolm's hustler friends, such as Sammy the Pimp, whose considerable business skills might have helped him build industries instead of a pimping empire. Similarly, West Indian Archie's photographic memory and quick math skills might have gotten him far in school instead of in gambling rackets. Malcolm's reference to the lofty career aspirations that form part of the American dream—probing space or curing cancer—underscores that these opportunities are not open to blacks, however. Instead, blacks, discouraged from pursuing any but the most menial jobs, can find a place for themselves in America only on the lowermost rungs of society.

2.   "Yes! Yes, that raping, red-headed devil was my
      grandfather! That close, yes! My mother's father! She didn't
      like to speak of it, can you blame her? She said she never laid
      eyes on him! She was glad for that! I'm glad for her! If I
      could drain away his blood that pollutes my body, and
      pollutes my complexion, I'd do it! Because I hate every drop
      of the rapist's blood that's in me!"

This passage from Chapter TWELVE, "Savior," an excerpt from one
of Malcolm's early speeches as a Nation of Islam minister, demonstrates the fierceness of his anti–white sentiment. The "raping, red-
headed devil" is Malcolm's grandfather, a white man on the Carib-
bean island of Antigua who fathered Malcolm's mother, Louise, by
raping her mother. Though the man is Malcolm's own grandfather,
Malcolm condemns him for his odious actions and for the oppression that he represents. In his youth, Malcolm does experience ben-
efits from having lighter skin, such as his father treating him well
and his easier time integrating into his white school. But such bene-
fits eventually only frustrate him because they illuminate the depths
of the real racial boundaries he faces.

Malcolm's agitation about "*his* blood pollut[ing] *my* body"
reflects his belief in the Nation of Islam's genetic theory of race,
which holds that white people were bred from black people by a
mad scientist in order to unleash evil on the world. The racist values
behind this attitude put Malcolm on a parallel with racist whites.
Furthermore, by dwelling on the rape of black women by white men
and the evils of interracial intercourse, Malcolm evokes the debate
on miscegenation, a term that denotes the mixing of races and that
racist whites use to denounce interracial sex as an attack on white
racial purity. While Malcolm's rhetoric is as fanatical as that of
white racists, we can easily understand it as a reaction to the white
rhetoric that oppresses his people. The unity he seeks among blacks
requires excluding whites, just as the unspoken unity among whites
requires excluding blacks. It is not surprising, then, that Malcolm
X's racism against whites has many of same characteristics as white
racism against blacks.

3. America needs to understand Islam, because this is the one religion that erases from its society the race problem.

In the course of recounting his pilgrimage in Chapter SEVENTEEN, "Mecca," Malcolm reveals his continued faith in Islam as a potential source for social change in America, but also reveals the difference between his experience of Middle Eastern Islam and the form of Islam he has practiced in the United States. While affiliated with the Nation of Islam, Malcolm uses Islam as a vehicle for promoting spiritual, social, political, and economic self-sufficiency among black people. Malcolm's is a simplified version of Islam, bent around demonizing whites and giving a rigid version of independence to black people. Later, in Mecca, at a time of personal upheaval and exile from the Nation of Islam, Malcolm discovers a much deeper Islam that is concerned with universal theological questions rather than with immediate political concerns. This quotation, steeped in the wisdom his experiences have given him, shows that Malcolm believes that America's race problem is resolvable. Malcolm bases his contention that Islam "erases from its society the race problem" on his experience of brotherhood in Mecca with white-skinned Muslims. His ability to live closely with them, without a trace of racial tension, enables him to see beyond the racial hierarchy of American society.

QUOTATIONS

4.   I reflected many, many times to myself upon how the American Negro has been entirely brainwashed from ever seeing or thinking of himself, as he should, as a part of the nonwhite peoples of the world.

This quote, made by Malcolm after his 1964 trip to Mecca and Africa, and recounted in Chapter Eighteen, "El-Hajj Malik El-Sha-bazz," shows the strength of his commitment to a broader perspective on race relations and oppression. While still blaming white people for the difficulties that black Americans face, Malcolm suggests a unified global black community as a potential remedy for the struggle of blacks everywhere. Unlike his claim that Islam can be a tool that helps all Americans redefine their understanding of race, Malcolm's perspective here focuses on building up black power rather than on expanding both whites' and blacks' perspective. His assertion that whites have "brainwashed" blacks in order to disempower them reflects his belief that blacks throughout the world must work together to overcome white oppression.

QUOTATIONS

5.   I've had enough of someone else's propaganda....I'm for
      truth, no matter who tells it. I'm for justice, no matter who it
      is for or against. I'm a human being first and foremost, and
      as such I'm for whoever and whatever benefits humanity as
      a whole.

This passage, from a letter Malcolm writes while in Mecca to some
American friends, appears in Chapter Nineteen, "1965," and
shows how Malcolm's understanding of America's race problems
has matured. He is no longer willing to submit unquestioningly to
the propaganda of "someone else"—namely Elijah Muhammad—
in deference to whom Malcolm has been squelching his own opinions for the past decade. Malcolm resists the Nation of Islam's anti-
white rhetoric and separatist tendencies, which he now sees as an
obstacle rather than an aid to progress. In a stunning reversal of pol-
icy, Malcolm broadens his work for racial equality by opening the
door to conversations with white people and collaborations with
white organizations.

   In committing to the abstract ideals of truth and justice, Malcolm
sets the stage to eclipse his status as a black political leader by
becoming a global political figure. However, while this letter does
signal a major change in Malcolm's perspective, his subsequent
actions do not necessarily back up his claims here. On returning to
New York City, for example, Malcolm receives a flood of requests
from white people to join his new organization. His rejection of
them on the grounds that whites must work with their own people
before attempting to form a coalition with blacks reveals limits to
his new outlook. Nevertheless, his openness to having white people
work for racial justice at all marks a step of progress from his earlier
belief that black people are the only ones who can improve black lives.

QUOTATIONS

KEY FACTS

FULL TITLE
The Autobiography of Malcolm X

AUTHOR
Alex Haley wrote the work based on his extensive interviews with Malcolm X.

TYPE OF WORK
Nonfiction

GENRE
Autobiography; memoir

LANGUAGE
English

DATE OF FIRST PUBLICATION
1965

PUBLISHER
Grove Press

NARRATOR
Malcolm tells his life story while he is in the last years of his life. Alex Haley recounts the end of Malcolm's life in the epilogue.

POINT OF VIEW
Malcolm speaks in the first person, focusing on his actions and thoughts at each point in his life. However, in each chapter he does include some opinions based on his current perspective late in his life. In the epilogue, Alex Haley speaks in the first person.

TONE
Malcolm alternates between simply presenting the events of his life and commenting on their social context. His tone ranges from matter-of-fact to angry.

TENSE
Past

SETTING (TIME)
1925–1965

SETTING (PLACE)

United States (Omaha, Lansing, Boston, New York, Chicago, and Detroit), the Middle East, and Africa

PROTAGONIST

Malcolm, who is known as Malcolm Little, Detroit Red, Malcolm X, and El-Hajj Malik El-Shabazz at various points in his life

MAJOR CONFLICT

Malcolm struggles against both the racism of white America and the internal problems of various civil rights organizations.

RISING ACTION

After the government tears apart his family and he can no longer bear the racism of his all-white high school in Michigan, Malcolm flees to Boston and Harlem, where he sinks deep into a life of crime.

CLIMAX

Malcolm's conversion to Islam in prison after long hours of studying puts him on a course to rise in the ranks of the Nation of Islam.

FALLING ACTION

After rising to fame as a fiery Muslim minister, Malcolm leaves the Nation of Islam to discover a more tolerant and global worldview.

THEMES

Malcolm's changing perspective on racism; the similarity between hustling and activism; humanity as a basic right

MOTIFS

Status symbols; travel and transformation

SYMBOLS

The conk; the watch, suitcase, and eyeglasses

FORESHADOWING

Malcolm's peaceful surrender to a Boston detective foreshadows his later submission to the Nation of Islam leader, Elijah Muhammad. Malcolm's description of his father's murder and his assertion that he too will die violently foreshadows his own assassination.

STUDY QUESTIONS & ESSAY TOPICS

STUDY QUESTIONS

1. *How does Malcolm X's understanding of racial identity change over the course of his life? Consider the different phases of Malcolm's life.*

During his life, Malcolm has as many attitudes toward his identity as he has names, and he experiences a significant transformation over the course of the autobiography. Early on, Malcolm learns that there is no way to escape his black identity. As a child he is called "nigger" so often that he believes it is his given name. At school in Lansing, he finds a social barrier between himself and white girls. Even as Malcolm earns top grades and is elected class president, a teacher discourages him from becoming a lawyer, because Malcolm is black, and teaches him racist propaganda. Malcolm leaves Michigan because he knows that he cannot escape the limiting racial identity that society imposes on him. In the Harlem underworld, Malcolm remakes himself in the lawless and isolated image of the black hustler. His few interactions with whites are shallow and exploitative: he uses his white girlfriend Sophia for status, just as she uses him; he bootlegs liquor for a Jewish nightclub owner; and he guides white men to black prostitutes.

After years of study in prison, Malcolm reconsiders his racial identity in the light of history and philosophy, and discovers answers to his questions about race in the pro-black rhetoric of the Nation of Islam. His acceptance of the Nation's belief that black people are an original and good people, and whites an aberration meant to spread evil in the world, reverses Malcolm's understanding of blacks and whites. Later, in Mecca, Malcolm learns to see beyond America's race problems even as he digs more firmly into his black identity. Feeling brotherhood with white-skinned Muslims, he returns to the United States with a message of racial tolerance and an impartial commitment to truth and justice. Still, he believes the most promising allies of American blacks are the oppressed, nonwhite peoples of the world, not American whites. Nevertheless, he has developed, by the end of his life, a broader perspective on racism. Though he initially interprets the hatred that whites direct toward him as a personal attack that he must fend off for himself, he now understands that racism is a worldwide force that all must unite to combat.

2.   *How does Malcolm X's view of white people change over the course of his life, and why? Consider the different phases of Malcolm's life.*

When Malcolm is a child, his parents teach him not to take abuse from white people. Although he is briefly happy while staying with the Swerlins, his white foster family, he is not content being their "mascot." When Malcolm moves to Boston, his sole significant contact with white people is Sophia, whom he never acknowledges as anything more than an object. Once he leaves Boston, Malcolm treats white people as they have always treated him: inhumanly. By the time Malcolm reaches prison, this impulse to treat white people as inhuman has been so reinforced by his experiences that he readily accepts Elijah Muhammad's teachings that the white man is the devil. When Malcolm reviews the white people he has known, he can think of only one, his Jewish boss, who treated him with any decency at all. From his moment of conversion to Islam until his falling out with the Nation of Islam, Malcolm upholds the party line that all whites are devils. On his trip to Mecca, however, Malcolm meets unprejudiced white Muslims and reconsiders the views he has held for so many years against whites. Malcolm comes to see white racism as the unfortunate product of particular circumstances rather than as an indication that white people are inherently evil.

3.   *What role do women play in the* AUTOBIOGRAPHY OF
     MALCOLM X?

Several women provide Malcolm crucial support in his endeavors, and he is grateful for their support of him. Malcolm remembers his mother, Louise, constantly cooking and caring for her children. She sacrifices much to provide for them and is driven mad in the end by her inability to do so. Malcolm's conscientious visits to her in the mental hospital show that he appreciates her commitment to him. Similarly, Ella, Malcolm's half-sister, often supports Malcolm at her own expense. After putting him up and finding him a job in Boston, for example, she later finances his trip to Mecca. Finally, though Malcolm's view of his wife, Betty, can seem unemotional at times, he appreciates her quiet strength.

However, many critics have claimed that the Malcolm X portrayed in the work is a misogynistic figure, and Malcolm's remarks on women provide ample evidence for this view. His claim to trust most women only twenty-five percent suggests that he subscribes to an unfair stereotype about women in the same way that many whites subscribe to unfair stereotypes about blacks. Malcolm treats the women he meets in his early adulthood, such as Laura and Sophia, as objects. After starting a promising relationship with Laura, who is black, Malcolm leaves her abruptly for an attractive white woman, Sophia. This act is more than simply a headstrong act of teenage disloyalty. It is a reflection of Malcolm's hunger for the status that goes along with being seen around town with a white woman. Malcolm's strong interest in fighting racial inequality does not translate into a strong interest in fighting gender inequality.

QUESTIONS & ESSAYS

SUGGESTED ESSAY TOPICS

1. Why does Malcolm go into the details of his early life in Michigan, Boston, and New York?

2. How do the lessons and skills of Malcolm's life on the street influence his demeanor as a political leader?

3. What, in Malcolm's experiences, draws him to an activism more militant than the nonviolent activism of Martin Luther King, Jr.?

4. In one speech about the need for blacks to identify with the nonwhite peoples of the world Malcolm X says, "You can't hate Africa and not hate yourself." What experiences lead him to make this statement?

REVIEW & RESOURCES

QUIZ

1. Where was Malcolm X born?

   A. Omaha, Nebraska
   B. Milwaukee, Wisconsin
   C. Lansing, Michigan
   D. Boston, Massachusetts

2. Why did white people murder Earl Little?

   A. He owed them money
   B. He slept with a white woman
   C. He was spreading the ideas of Marcus Garvey
   D. He was a Muslim

3. With whom does Malcolm live in Lansing?

   A. The Gohannases
   B. The Swerlins
   C. The Lyons
   D. The Fords

4. In eighth grade, what does Malcolm declare he wishes to become?

   A. A doctor
   B. A teacher
   C. A preacher
   D. A lawyer

5. Who does Malcolm first meet in Boston after he moves in with Ella?

   A. Sammy the Pimp
   B. West Indian Archie
   C. Shorty
   D. Sophia

6. Where does Malcolm land his first job in Boston?

    A.   The Savoy Ballroom
    B.   The Roseland State Ballroom
    C.   Small's Paradise
    D.   The Apollo Theater

7. Who raises Laura?

    A.   The Swerlins
    B.   Her mother
    C.   Her half-sister
    D.   Her grandmother

8. Why does Malcolm leave Laura?

    A.   She is too wild
    B.   He starts dating a white woman
    C.   She doesn't like dancing
    D.   Ella prohibits Malcolm from seeing her

9. Why does Malcolm first get a railroad job?

    A.   He hopes to see New York
    B.   He wants to avoid the draft
    C.   He is determined to earn the respect of white people
    D.   He plans on selling reefers to traveling musicians

10. What is Malcolm's first job in New York?

    A.   Drug dealer
    B.   Waiter at Small's Paradise
    C.   Shoeshine boy at the Savoy Ballroom
    D.   Pimp

11. In Harlem, by what name does Malcolm become known?

    A.   Lansing Slim
    B.   Little the Pimp
    C.   Detroit Red
    D.   Satan

12. How does Malcolm initially try to evade the narcotics squad?

    A.   By moving his business around
    B.   By selling reefers on the railroad
    C.   By changing his hours
    D.   By selling through the mail

13. Of what does West Indian Archie accuse Malcolm?

    A.   Selling bad dope
    B.   Sleeping with his girlfriend
    C.   Collecting on a number he didn't bet on in a lottery
    D.   Violating the codes of the Nation of Islam

14. How does Malcolm decide to support himself after he moves back to Boston?

    A.   By dealing drugs
    B.   By gambling
    C.   Through burglary
    D.   By attending college

15. At Massachusetts State Prison, what do the other inmates call Malcolm?

    A.   "X"
    B.   "Satan"
    C.   "Detroit Red"
    D.   "Little"

16. Who converts Malcolm to Islam?

    A.   Elijah Muhammad
    B.   Ella
    C.   Philbert
    D.   Reginald

17. Where does Malcolm go after being released from prison?

    A.   Boston
    B.   New York
    C.   Detroit
    D.   Chicago

REVIEW & RESOURCES

18. Where does Malcolm first see Elijah Muhammad?

    A.   In a vision
    B.   At a dinner at Wilfred's house
    C.   At a rally in New York
    D.   At a meeting in Chicago

19. What is Malcolm's first official post in the Nation of Islam?

    A.   The assistant minister at the Detroit temple
    B.   The first National Minister
    C.   The founder of the Boston temple
    D.   The head minister of the New York temple

20. Who is Malcolm X's future wife?

    A.   A white woman
    B.   A minister at the Boston temple
    C.   A teacher at the New York temple
    D.   A jazz singer

21. On which program does the Nation of Islam first appear on network television?

    A.   *The Hate that Hate Produced*
    B.   *The Black Muslims in America*
    C.   *Violence and Negroes*
    D.   *Self-Determination and Equal Rights for Blacks*

22. What is Malcolm shocked to learn that Elijah Muhammad has done?

    A.   Embezzled funds
    B.   Committed adultery
    C.   Broken the prohibition on alcohol
    D.   Spoken to the white media

23. After breaking with the Nation of Islam, what organization does Malcolm X found?

    A. The Southern Christian Leadership Conference
    B. The National Association for the Advancement of Colored People
    C. Muslim Mosque, Inc.
    D. The Universal Negro Improvement Association

24. What does Malcolm do to his hair in order to blend into white society?

    A. He conks it
    B. He bleaches it
    C. He shaves it off
    D. He parts it to one side

25. Toward the end of his life, what does Malcolm believe?

    A. That he will live to a ripe old age
    B. That people will remember him for his change in viewpoint
    C. That he will die a violent death
    D. That he will reconcile with the Nation of Islam

REVIEW & RESOURCES

ANSWER KEY:
1: A; 2: C; 3: B; 4: D; 5: C; 6: B; 7: D; 8: B; 9: A; 10: B; 11: C;
12: A; 13: C; 14: C; 15: B; 16: D; 17: C; 18: D; 19: A; 20: C; 21: C; 22: B; 23: C; 24: A; 25: C

SUGGESTIONS FOR FURTHER READING

APPIAH, KWAME ANTHONY, and HENRY LOUIS GATES, JR., eds. *Africana: The Encyclopedia of the African and African-American Experience.* New York: Perseus Books Group, 1999.

BALDWIN, JAMES. *The Fire Next Time.* New York: Laurel, 1963.

———. *One Day, When I Was Lost: A Screenplay.* New York: Dial Press, 1973.

BREITMAN, GEORGE, ed. *Malcolm X Speaks.* New York: Pathfinder, 1965.

CLARK, STEVE, ed. *Malcolm X Talks to Young People.* New York: Pathfinder, 1965.

GOLDMAN, PETER. *The Death and Life of Malcolm X.* Chicago: University of Illinois Press, 1979.

JENKINS, ROBERT, ed. *The Malcolm X Encyclopedia.* Westport, Connecticut: Greenwood, 2002.

STRICKLAND, WILLIAM. *Malcolm X, Make It Plain.* New York: Viking, 1994.

REVIEW & RESOURCES

SPARKNOTES
TEST PREPARATION
GUIDES

The SparkNotes team figured it was time to cut standardized tests down to size. We've studied the tests for you, so that SparkNotes test prep guides are:

Smarter
Packed with critical-thinking skills and test-
taking strategies that will improve your score.

Better
Fully up to date, covering all new features of the tests,
with study tips on every type of question.

Faster
Our books cover exactly what you need to
know for the test. No more, no less.

SparkNotes Guide to the SAT & PSAT
SparkNotes Guide to the SAT & PSAT — Deluxe Internet Edition
SparkNotes Guide to the ACT
SparkNotes Guide to the ACT — Deluxe Internet Edition
SparkNotes SAT Verbal Workbook
SparkNotes SAT Math Workbook
SparkNotes Guide to the SAT II Writing
5 More Practice Tests for the SAT II Writing
SparkNotes Guide to the SAT II U.S. History
5 More Practice Tests for the SAT II History
SparkNotes Guide to the SAT II Math Ic
5 More Practice Tests for the SAT II Math Ic
SparkNotes Guide to the SAT II Math IIc
5 More Practice Tests for the SAT II Math IIc
SparkNotes Guide to the SAT II Biology
5 More Practice Tests for the SAT II Biology
SparkNotes Guide to the SAT II Physics

SAT and PSAT are registered trademarks of the College Entrance Examination Board, which does not endorse these books.
ACT is a registered trademark of ACT, Inc. which neither sponsors nor endorses these books.

SparkNotes Literature Guides